Young Ladies Who
L. E. A. D.

Learn. **E**xcel. **A**chieve. **D**are to be great.

Presented by

Dr. Sharon H. Porter

Foreword by

Christen Elizabeth (Lizzie) Funderburk

Featuring

Um'Bria Adams

Lauren Baldwin

Kaylee Mayhew

Sydney Porter

Alesha Wilson

Tahjai Renee Ward

Copyright © 2020 Perfect Time SHP LLC

All rights reserved. No portion of this book may be reproduced, stored in a retrieval system, or transmitted in any form or by any means—electronic, mechanical, photocopy recording, scanning, or other—except for brief quotations without the prior written permission of the author.

Perfect Time SHP LLC

info@perfecttimeshp.com

www.perfecttimeshppublishing.com

ISBN: 978-1-7347783-4-2

Ordering Information:

Bulk Sales: Special discounts are available on quantity purchases by organizations, associations, and nonprofits. For details, contact the publisher at the aforementioned email address.

Published by Perfect Time SHP LLC

DEDICATION

This book in its entirety is dedicated to **Chloe, Nyla, Layla, Kaylee, Ryleigh, Elle, Shekinah, Imani, Tylic, and Um'Bria**. You all come from a long line of strong Women Who Lead. You are incredibly talented and the future is certainly yours. Set your goals, plan, strategize, and execute. You can do and be ANYTHING! I look forward to seeing it all materialize.

This book is also dedicated to **Eva Woods Harris and her daughters; Mary, Joann, Luzelle, and Ruby, Mamie Word Hargro and her daughter, Ida Mae.**

I L.E.A.D. because of YOU.

CHAPTER DEDICATIONS

Um'Bria Adams

My chapter is dedicated to the loving memory of Antavis "Ty" Johnson Your encouraging words and constant motivation throughout the years have pushed me to heights I never thought were possible.

Your life was truly a blessing, you are loved far beyond words, and you will be missed beyond measure. I love you Ty, thank you for inspiring me to be great.

Lauren Baldwin

My chapter is dedicated to every child striving to achieve greatness in any and all forms. Never give up, and always trust yourself. You know you best.

Also, I would like to dedicate this chapter to my mother who has never stopped believing in me, no matter what.

Kaylee Mayhew

My chapter is dedicated to "My Tribe". You have been there for me every step of the way. I appreciate you… I LOVE you!

Sydney Porter

I would like to dedicate my chapter to all the beautiful little brown skin girls that aspire and dream to be great in this world. Do not allow the outside world to tell you cannot accomplish your goals because I am here to tell you it can be done and it will be done.

Remember to always be yourself because your differences make you unique and that's special. You are beautiful inside and out continue to be a light of hope in a world of confusion.

Alesha Wilson

To my village.

Thank you for the support, the recharge, the reassurance, the laughs, the hugs, the calls, and your steadfast energy. Most importantly thank you for believing in me.

My chapter is dedicated to Rashad, Melyssa, and Jaydin for fueling me through this process and elevating my reason. Love.

Tahjai Renee Ward

I would like to thank all of my family and friends who have supported and encouraged me to go on with faith!

CONTENTS

Acknowledgments i

Foreword iii

Introduction 9

Advice to Young Women – Um'Bria Adams 13

Learning to Lead – Lauren Baldwin 21

Natural Born Leader – Kaylee Mayhew 29

The Growth of a Young Lady – Sydney N. Porter 36

Imperfect Leader – Alesha Wilson 52

But God – Tahjai Renee Ward 62

About the Visionary Author 71

ACKNOWLEDGMENTS

I would like to thank the **Young Ladies Who L.E.A.D.** contributing authors; **Um'Bria Adams, Lauren Baldwin, Kaylee Mayhew, Sydney Porter, Alesha Wilson, Tahjai Renee Ward**, and the Foreword Author, **Christen Elizabeth (Lizzie) Funderburk** for saying YES!!

You are Young Ladies who are **L**earning, **E**xcelling, **A**chieving, and **D**aring to be great…

You are indeed Young Ladies Who **L.E.A.D.**

Foreword

Growing up, I always considered a leader someone that tells others what to do, but that is far from what a true leader really is. When I think of the definition of a leader, it is someone that is loving and empathetic, passionate and driven, and authentic. Being a leader means that you are intentional about positively impacting your audience through your gift. We are all blessed with a gift or talent upon entering the world. When we find our calling, I believe that each one of us has the duty to pour back into others. That is a true leader.

I consider my most effective leadership skill to be building relationships. These days it is so hard to find a genuine connection. It's never about what others can do for you, but what we can do for others. Leaders long to leave a lasting impression on everyone they come into contact with. I knew that I was called to be a leader when I realized that I would never fit in trying to be someone that I knew God hadn't called me to be.

The vision for starting my business came to me in August 2014 when I was a college undergrad student looking for ways to save money so I decided to make my own laundry detergent. I made my first five gallon batch which lasted the entire semester between me and three other roommates (and we still had some left). I even had other people tell me that they would pay me to make it for them. I could not believe that people actually wanted ME to make this product for them AND they were willing to pay ME. The real drive came about when I started getting testimonials about how my laundry detergent was actually helping others improve their skin. This made me keep going because I felt like people needed me. I knew I had found my calling in life.

Starting my business has to be one of the scariest things I have ever done in my life. I am a leader because I stepped out on faith, and I bet on myself with no startup money and no business plan. All I had was a vision. I am a leader because I encourage and help other women to also follow and reach their dreams. When I started my business, I told God that by year five, I wanted to make six figures, and I did. I told God that I wanted to help others be their best self by making people feel good about the skin they were in, I did and still do to this day. I also told him that I wanted to move my business out of my basement, and he gave me an entire studio to create my products and a store to sell my products. Not only did I speak those things into existence, I worked my butt off because when

I set a goal for myself, I don't stop until I reach it.

See, the thing about me is that I do not like to lose. When I began this journey, I knew it would not be easy, but I did it anyway. There are plenty of companies out there doing the same thing I am doing, but what makes me different is my passion and my determination. I always want more for myself. I do not allow anyone to make me feel bad about evolving or wanting more or doing something that will make me better. Being my best self is what makes me unique. I always ask myself, out of all the places my customers could have shopped...why my products? Why my business? I realized that people enjoyed the way I made them feel...loved and important, well because they are.

Since being in business, I have faced many obstacles. I think the biggest one I have been faced with is just trying to prove myself because I'm young. Not only am I young, but I am also a black female so I always feel like I have to work ten times harder. Although this is an obstacle, I always try to look at the glass half full, not half empty. This challenge will only make me stronger in the end because by working harder, I am also becoming more tenacious and determined to achieve every goal I have set for myself and then some.

Through this journey, one thing I have learned (and still learning) is how to delegate more. As a woman that leads, I often feel like I have to wear multiple hats to ensure tasks get done properly. Good leaders know that they cannot reach success alone. I am learning that asking for help doesn't mean I am weak, but that I'm strong enough to ask in the first place. As women, we do so much and play so many different roles. Asking for help and trusting others to help me are things I am still working on to this day.

The young women that have contributed to this collaboration project all demonstrate great leadership. What an amazing example for young ladies everywhere. It is extremely important for all of us to share what we learn, how we achieve and excel. We simply must all dare to be great. Greatness is in each of us. Sometimes we don't always see it or feel it. That's when the village steps in. We have to lift each other up and help each other see the greatness in ourselves.

To young ladies everywhere, I believe in you. I believe in what you have to offer to the world. Stand up and be proud of who you are and all that you accomplish in life. Never dim your light because of the discomfort of others. Shine bright always.

Christen Elizabeth (Lizzie) Funderburk
Owner and CEO
Lizzie's all-natural Products, LLC

About Christen Elizabeth "Lizzie" Funderburk

Christen Elisabeth (Lizzie) Funderburk, a North Carolina Native began her entrepreneurial journey in 2015 when she founded her first company Lizzie's Laundry Detergent which is now known as Lizzie's All-natural Products LLC. Christen's lifelong battle with eczema is one of the main reasons she started this company.

For Christen, having eczema used to mean sleepless nights, waking up to new scars, wearing long clothing to hide her skin and just being flat out self-conscious and ashamed of who she was because of her eczema. Although eczema is not curable, it is treatable and over the years Christen has learned that healing our bodies through the power of nature is real. Her mission is to help others feel good in the skin they are in and build confidence.

Christen is a 2014 alumna of The University of North Carolina at Pembroke with a major in Criminal Justice and minor in Sociology. Currently, Christen is pursuing her esthetician license so she can fulfill her dream of opening an all-natural spa one day to cater to people and their natural skincare needs.

Besides helping others, Christen enjoys watching a good crime show, reading, thrifting, anything skincare, hiking, eating chipotle, and long bike rides on her cruiser.

Introduction

Young Ladies Who L.E.A.D. is a mentoring program I founded for girls (young ladies) in elementary school, grades 2nd-4th grade. Why 2nd 4th grade, you ask? Between the ages of seven and nine is when peer acceptance becomes more important than ever before. It is also the age when a sense of body image has begun. It is a developmentally critical time in the lives of young ladies.

I have served as a mentor for many organizations that mentors middle school and high school students. Without a doubt, that group of young ladies definitely benefits from strong mentors. But as an elementary school principal, I see the self-doubt and lack of confidence in many of the female students at an early age.

Young Ladies Who L.E.A.D, the book collaboration, exemplifies all that I want my elementary students to see, feel, and experience. These five young ladies have been hand-selected to share how they **L**earn, **E**xcel, **A**chieve, and **D**are to be great… (**LEAD**). They are indeed leading in their careers, their businesses, and most importantly, their lives.

I need my little great nieces to know that they can be and do ANYTHING their little minds and hearts desire. Little girls everywhere, should see the possibilities and the probabilities around them and even think beyond what they can see. Yes, anything is possible.., but I want them to know that it is also probable... Possible refers to what *can* be ...Probable refers to what is *likely* to be....

I need young ladies to begin setting SMARTER GOALS., not just SMART goals, but smartER... goals...Add excitement and relevance to your goal-setting. Leading is extremely important to me. When it comes to leading, I always say "lead where you are". We know that leadership is not about the title or position you have, it is all about the influence and impact you have on others and in situations. Now more than ever, it is imperative that we start our young ladies off in life being leaders.; expressing themselves, standing up for what they believe, and taking initiative. We can no longer wait for others to exert themselves as leaders. "The future is female"...Go LEAD!

My all-time favorite Young Lady Who L.E.A.D. to date is Malala Yousafzai. Malala is the teenager from Pakistan who survived a gunshot wound in the head for standing up for her right to education. Her story truly inspired me. At sixteen, Malala became a symbol of leadership. She is the youngest recipient for the Nobel Peace Prize and truly is a Young Lady

Introduction

Who L.E.A.D.

Young Ladies, know your value….Know your worth, and continue to Learn, Excel, Achieve, and Dare to be great…Continue to LEAD!

Um'Bria Adams

"Don't allow others to decide your happiness…" -
Um'Bria Adams

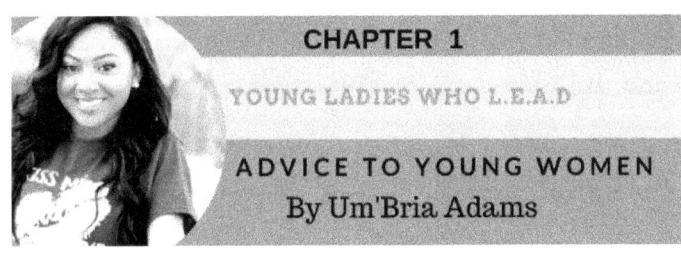

ADVICE TO YOUNG WOMEN

By Um'Bria Adams

I want to say that I am truly blessed to have this opportunity to share my life's aspirations and goals with young ladies. Every young woman should be self-driven and should also set both their own personal goals and life aspirations. You have the freedom to choose what you would like to make of yourself. Your life and a dream or goal starts you on that journey. Every individual's dreams and goals are different in life; however, some basic goals can be the same. Some basic goals that are the same include graduating high school or getting a good paying job. What sets our journeys and paths apart from each other are the choices we make to graduate or what job we choose to take. Even our drive, ambition, and personalities set each individual apart from the rest of the world, when it comes to making goals.

My goals and ambitions start off simple as well; however, they expand and narrow for my life goals to be achieved. One of my current basic life goals and ambitions is to overcome failure. From experience, failures in life can be the reasons why a person gives up. Growing up, I was able to overcome my failures by seeing them as an opportunity to grow as a young woman. When I was younger, my mother introduced me to a quote by Michael Jordan, *"I can accept failure, everyone fails at something. But I can't accept not trying."* From this quote, I have learned that when you fall, you have to get up and try again. To everyone, failure should be a reason to try harder until you succeed. Another one of my basic life goals is to learn to let go of the toxic people that found their way into my life.

Having a toxic person in your life can be unavoidable. Throughout high school, I came across many toxic relationships, whether it was a friend or boyfriend. Those toxic relationships not only stressed me out, but it also had a major impact on my long-term goals. Eliminating these individuals from my life was hard, but afterwards, I felt so much better. The lessons that I have learned from these toxic relationships are to never be too nice, learn to set boundaries, and always put your own happiness first. Being too nice can result in someone taking you for granted. Individuals who are too nice are sometimes afraid to say no. Nice can oftentimes be considered a weakness when you set yourself up to be taken advantage of. Setting personal boundaries is important simply because they reveal specific guidelines of how you want to be treated by others. Boundaries can also be seen as a way to establish the behaviors of others around you. Putting your happiness first is important. Don't allow others to decide your happiness, because only you know what makes you the happiest you. Putting yourself first is not wrong; everyone should find a way to balance both time spent with others with quality time to themselves.

A few of my expanded goals in life are to gain balance, to be financially stable, and to be married and have harmony in both my marriage and family. To be able to have balance in work, school, and family is what I mean by gaining balance. To achieve this goal, I will start by bettering my priorities. Being able to create time for the things that I **have** to do and things that I **like** to do is balance. When an individual gains balance, it strengthens both your mental and emotional health.

Every woman, young or old needs to have balance in life. The choices I make help me balance my life to achieve everything that I want out of life. Being financially stable can be difficult, but it also makes life go on so much smoother. Me being an independent individual, I have never liked to ask anyone for anything. Being able to better manage my finances would be a great accomplishment for me. In order to better manage my finances, I have started cutting down on my spending habits and I have also started saving a set amount of my income. I made this one of my many goals because I find it easier to achieve goals when they are set in advance.

Getting married and having harmony in both my marriage and family is an important expanded goal for me. Seeing my mom go through what she went through as a single mother allowed me to realize that every relationship requires harmony. To achieve a harmonious relationship, I will be sure that me and the person can see eye to eye without any argument or disagreements. Adding on to having a harmonious marriage, having a harmonious family is important to me as well. When a family can function without anyone not wanting to be around each other, or without being distant is what I visualize when I think of harmony in a family. I have been in various situations that have taught me many life lessons, both good and bad. One of the many life lessons I have learned is that everyone is not your friend. In life, I've come across many long lasting friendships, along with some that did not last, due to them not being there when I needed them most. Just because someone likes to hang around you and laugh with you does not mean they are your friend. There was a time where I shared one of my biggest secrets with a friend; That "friend" soon went and told many people that same secret. Although I was devastated that people other than her knew that secret, I realized that real situations can reveal fake people. Another life lesson that I would like to share with young ladies is that bad things will happen in life and there is absolutely no way around it. There will be many unfortunate things to happen in your life, you just have to be strong and those hard times will pass. I have also learned to always live life to the fullest, you only live once. Growing up, I have been taught that every day is not promised to anyone. In my opinion, living life to the fullest means to take risks, tell your loved ones that you love them daily, and make the most of each day. Last but certainly not least, always remember that your voice matters. Coming from me, an individual who is very shy and hesitant when it comes to speaking up. I have learned that if you believe in something, speak up and voice your opinion. Speaking up can change a lot in the way others view a situation; with that being said, always remember that you deserve to be heard.

To every young lady reading this, I would like to give several pieces of advice. When going into college, pick a major that is right for you. Throughout high school, I told myself that I wanted to become a doctor, simply because of the amount of income they received. My senior year, I had the opportunity to shadow a doctor, and from that experience I realized that particular field of study just wasn't for me. There are many individuals who take on majors based on their income, but is that really something you want to spend the rest of your life doing? After asking myself that same question, I knew that I liked sports, and working with kids, which led me to my top two fields of study, exercise science and early childhood education. With that being said, I advise every young woman to follow your dreams and to take full advantage of your career advisors. Another piece of advice I would like to give is to never allow anyone to tell you, you can't do something. When someone says you're not that, you say I am that. When someone says you are that, you say I am not that.

About Um'Bria Adams

Um'Bria Adams was born on November 28, 2000, in Anderson SC. She graduated from Westside High School in the year 2019 and is currently enrolled at Tricounty Technical College. Um'Bria's major is Exercise Science, in which she plans to use her degree to become an occupational therapist. Since 2018, Um'Bria is employed by Ingles Markets.

Um'Bria is the daughter of Roshonda Johnson and the sister of two younger brothers, Kiantae and Kendrell. She was born in Anderson SC and resided in Iva during her early childhood.

Um'Bria has been through many trials and tribulations, in her life, and is proud to share a piece of how she gained a sense of balance throughout her journey.

Lauren Baldwin

"Stay true to yourself and your beliefs" -Lauren Baldwin

CHAPTER 2
YOUNG LADIES WHO L.E.A.D
LEARNING TO LEAD
By: Lauren Baldwin

LEARNING TO LEAD

By: Lauren Baldwin

I believe I became a leader when I decided to stop thinking of learning as a way to hoard information for my own gain, but as a way to enrich the lives of others through shared knowledge. That was the day I decided to become a teacher.

When I became an educator, I knew I wanted to help make a positive impact in the lives of children, but most especially to those children who so often get overlooked; and therefore, rarely get a fighting chance. Which is why when I chose to make my career in education, I specifically chose to be an educator to individuals with learning and behavioral challenges. Even though I've only been in my field for a few years, I can honestly say that no other job has fulfilled the way teaching has. I'm a person who needs to feel emotionally invested in whatever I set my mind to. I need to be passionate about a task, otherwise I lose interest because there's no substance involved for me. I'm most passionate about learning. All my life I've loved school because it gave me the opportunity to learn new things, and I looked up to a lot of my teachers as mentors because they not only taught me things that were helpful and helped me succeed in school, but they ultimately gave me great tools that I could use to succeed in my everyday life. Some of my greatest teachers are truly the reason my passion for learning ultimately became a love for teaching.

Being an educator has helped me see myself as a leader because I can see the positive impact my actions have had on many students. I've been able to help guide them in directions that they themselves didn't believe possible, simply because I believe in them and encourage them to believe in themselves and their capabilities. Many of my students have learning disabilities that make things more challenging from time to time, and a lot of them have had teachers in the past that haven't always been able to help them reach their full potential. However, with me as a teacher, most of my students have not only been able to graduate with their high school diploma, but have also been able to acquire internships, jobs, and even have been able to explore going to college. To me this is one of the greatest feelings because it lets me know that I was able to successfully help my students actualize their goals and send them into the world with the knowledge they need to help them thrive.

I believe one of my most effective leadership skills is my ability to seek first to understand, rather than to be understood. For me, it's been the intent to listen to understand rather than listening with the intent to reply that has really helped me not only in my career, but in my everyday life. When you seek to understand, you not only affirm the other person and what they have to say, but you actually are able to learn about them on a deeper level. Being able to empathize with others is important in any leadership position because it increases the levels of trust between all involved. People will feel as if they can come to you and be heard and understood. This skill has proven very effective in my career as a special needs' educator. My job is all about understanding my students and making sure they know they can trust me to help them succeed at anything they set their minds to. Whenever my students are having difficulties, I always encourage them to come to me and explain what's holding them back or giving them trouble. By listening to them with the intent to understand, I'm able to see things from their perspective and offer them a solution that is specific to their personal needs. By doing this, I show them that I have their best interest at heart and that they can confide in me whenever they feel lost or overwhelmed. Knowing that I'm there to help them succeed gives my students the confidence they need to do and be their absolute best, in school and in life after school.

One of the newer leadership skills I've gained has been better communication. Teachers are tasked with motivating, and instructing their students, and if you're a poor communicator, it's difficult to accomplish either. Being a good communicator is important in any position of leadership, but I've found it particularly useful as a teacher. By practicing good communication, I've been able to ensure that my students and I work as a team to navigate problems and resolve conflicts more effectively by being able to confide in one another and know that they're being not just heard but understood.

I've been able to overcome challenges by really learning to not only listen to myself, but to *trust* myself as well. Trusting myself and trusting my process and not comparing my journey to anyone else's has been the key to overcoming obstacles for me. It seems cliché, and also easier said than done, but like anything, practice makes perfect. I start small by asking myself what's holding me back. Once I fully understand the issue it's easier to develop a plan to overcome it. I try to be honest with myself about what I want and what it will realistically take to get me there. That's where the other important part comes in, which is, putting in the work. Believing you can do something isn't the same as actually doing it. Once I have my plan outlined, I carry it out with confidence. Sometimes I succeed and sometimes I fail, but I believe it's important to reflect on wins and losses in order to understand that each can be a learning opportunity as well as a potential steppingstone.

The main thing that has led to my "greatness" I would have to say, is my ability to remain open minded. I tend to look at things from many different perspectives other than my own, in order to get a more authentic understanding of other people and/or situations. This has helped me see success in my career as an educator by allowing me to be able to adapt to different behaviors quickly and rather than reacting to them, I am able to better understand what their thought process might be and I'm able to better assist my students with any challenges they may be facing. Being open minded makes me unique in a way because many people have a rigid way of thinking. To a lot of people things are either black or white with no room for gray areas. To me however, the gray areas are the spaces that intrigue me most. Gray areas allow for nuance which allows for deeper understanding on a more personal level and I believe my ability to seek deeper meaning and better understanding of the world around me has helped shape me into the person I am today.

I am incredibly proud of all of my accomplishments, starting with graduating from Westlake High School in 2008. I received recognition for having the highest individual fundraiser for local heroes while working as Community Ambassador for Mission BBQ. I raised over $10,000 for this great cause. I am currently pursuing a degree in education at the University of Maryland.

If I could offer young girls any advice, it would be to stay true to yourself and your beliefs. Always listen to yourself when making decisions and never let other people's opinions of you define you.

About Lauren Baldwin

Lauren Baldwin has always been passionate about learning. Which is why it was no surprise that she took a career in education. As a special education paraprofessional, Lauren feels she has finally found a career that not only fulfills her, but actively seeks to better the lives of the individuals she works with. She has been able to help multiple students reach their goal of not only earning their high school diploma, but also has been fortunate to be able to find her students internships, jobs, and higher education opportunities after graduation.

She believes that everyone is entitled to a quality education, and the opportunity to be the best they can be. Lauren knows that there is no single approach that works for everyone, so she continues to educate herself on the different types and aspects of learning and behavioral challenges in order to provide the most comprehensive and individualized learning strategies that work best for each of her students.

Lauren received her education at the University of Maryland where she majored in journalism before continuing her studies at Prince George's Community College where she majored in education.

Lauren is currently working as a paraprofessional at The Kennedy School in Washington D.C.

Kaylee Mayhew

"Don't follow the crowd… Be your own person"
~Kaylee Mayhew

Natural Born Leader

By: Kaylee Mayhew

I have always been a natural leader. I have never been one to play into what's popular. I like going with the flow. I like what I like...period. I don't let others influence what I do. I am an independent thinker and I take charge of my own choices. This is what I consider to be a leader.

Leadership Is…
I believe the difference between leading and managing are the sought outcomes of each. The main focus of a leader is making sure that the people are being edified. The main focus of a manager is making sure all bases are being covered in order to ensure the success of their business or whatever project is being worked on. In order to effectively lead you have to be an effective communicator; it is one of the most important skills as a leader. It's not always what you say, but more often, how

you say it that makes the difference. With proper communication there is no grey area....no confusion. Without confusions on ideas and feelings, tasks are able to be completed in a timely manner with minimal frustration. As a leader, effective communication also means being a great listener; especially when you are collaborating on a project. You must be able to listen and take in the ideas of others. It shows not only that you are open to new ideas but also that you are willing to integrate those ideas into the task at hand.

Effective listening and communication also helps to make you an overall well-rounded person because you are able to incorporate new ideas and skills into your own personal "bank" of knowledge that you can draw upon in other situations.

There are always going to be challenges and some of those challenges cannot be overcome alone. Leaders are not afraid to ask for assistance when needed! You should always let someone know when you are struggling. No one is perfect and has it all together. Showing and being open about those vulnerabilities and imperfections makes others feel as though they can relate to you more. Sometimes the people being led forget that the leaders are also human at the end of the day.

My Major Is…

I am in my senior year in college and I have changed my major THREE times! My first major was Elementary Education and Special Education. I then switched to Speech Pathology, and finally landed with Recreational Therapy. I come from a long line of educators, but this was not the reason I chose Education as my initial major. Ever since I was a little girl, playing with baby dolls, I loved kids and saw myself, one day, working with kids in some capacity. Education was simply the most natural way I thought I could achieve my ultimate goal. I soon realized I did not want to be stuck in a routine of working in a classroom and following a specific curriculum. I then changed my major to Speech Pathology because I have always been fascinated with communication and the different ways that humans of different abilities can learn to communicate. The major ended up being too math and science based so I went back to the drawing board frustrated that I hadn't found a major but knowing that the perfect major was out there for me. I met with a general advisor and she asked me what I liked to do. I told her that I liked playing with kids and I love individuals with special needs. I also shared with her that even though it sounded crazy, ultimately that my dream job is playing with kids. She told me she had just the major for me which was Recreational Therapy and I have been in love with my major ever since.

Class of 2015

As I think back on all I have accomplished thus far in life, I would have to say that graduating high school a year early is my greatest accomplishment to date. I was eager to get out of high school; I never really was a social butterfly in high school. I went to class, was on the Speech and Debate Team, and played softball. Beyond that, I wasn't really into cliques. I met with my high school advisor and we came up with a game plan. I had to take classes online and in person simultaneously and I would have to take a full course load online for two summers. During my "junior/senior" year, I was taking my junior classes at North Mecklenburg High School and my senior classes online. I did this while still playing softball and being on the Speech and Debate team.

Family Is…

I am who I am because of my family. My family's support has meant everything to me. My mom has always stood behind and beside me; even through the process of me finding my major. She has always been supportive in every decision I make. Not only my mom, but my entire family. I call them my tribe because it really does take a village to keep yourself going. Family is everything.

Who Am I?

I am a genuinely sweet and kind person. I see the good in everyone. I just want to help and love everybody, despite my own personal challenges and circumstances. I try not to let that affect who I am at my core. I was diagnosed with Generalized Anxiety, Insomnia and Depression my freshman year of high school. Initially, I was seeing a psychologist, but realized I wasn't getting what I needed. I had a genuine chemical imbalance and just talking to a therapist was not going to be enough. I was referred to a psychiatrist and was able to get the medication I needed to help manage my mental health. Slowly but surely, everything is working itself out and being open about suffering from mental health issues is a big part of my healing process. On top of taking medication I have taken an interest in yoga and finding other outlets to help me with my mental health.

My advice to younger ladies is to stay on top of your mental health. If you need help seek it and know that you are not alone in your struggles. We all need someone to talk to at some point, even if you are not suffering from mental health problems. Don't follow the crowd and be your own person. As you get older you will come to appreciate it and people will come to appreciate that about you.

About Kaylee Mayhew

Kaylee Mayhew is a senior at the University of North Carolina at Greensboro, studying Parks and Recreation Management with a concentration in Recreational Therapy. She was born and raised in Charlotte, North Carolina and is currently 21-years of age. Her faith, family, friends, and struggle with her mental health have helped her to develop into the woman and leader she is today.

She has a heart for children and people in general and openly seeks to help those in need. Her goal when helping others' is to always be the person that she did not have when she needed it. She believes that the best leaders lead by empowering and takes this approach in any situation that requires her leadership.

Sydney N. Porter

"Be yourself at all times..." ~Sydney N. Porter

CHAPTER 4

YOUNG LADIES WHO L.E.A.D

THE GROWTH OF A YOUNG LADY
By: Sydney N. Porter

THE GROWTH OF A YOUNG LADY

By: Sydney N. Porter

I define leadership as the act of organizing and guiding a person or people to positive solutions in order to solve a current problem or problems. Successful leadership involves effective communication, listening skills, and confidence in your own skills and knowledge. My leadership skills start with my interpersonal skills and confidence. I have the ability to connect with all kinds of people through all walks of life. Leadership begins within, taking your own skills and using them to organize, communicate, and find effective solutions.

When I am faced with a problem or a challenge, I never run or back down, but I find creative solutions to each and every issue that may arise. The art of being a true leader is to address challenges head on and to work through those challenges in order to garner positive results. I utilize this leadership skill on a daily basis within my professional life and my personal life. I have even been able to start consulting on the side using this skill. Having strong leadership skills can help propel you forward in your career. For example, during college and after college, I used to be a hostess. During my time as a hostess, I worked at four different restaurants, and at each restaurant, I always found myself in a leadership position of some sort. Sometimes, I would volunteer for these positions. Other times, I was promoted into them because my manager saw my leadership skills and my ability to lead/train our hostess staff effectively. The restaurant where I saw my leadership skills acknowledged and rewarded the most was when I worked at Ocean Prime Seafood and Steakhouse. Before I begin my story, I wanted to start off by saying that working at Ocean Prime was the best restaurant experience I have ever had, and if I had the chance to work with the company again I would. Now back to the story. Working at Ocean Prime was supposed to be temporary until I got a "real job" as I would like to say. I started out as a guest services hostess working on a team of ten other hostesses. We went through a long, two week training before we officially opened. The first month or so of being open was tough. We lost staff, and hours were slim because there were so many of us working. Even through that, I made sure I was always on time, I communicated effectively with management, and I put everything we were taught to practice.

This was my first restaurant using a real seating system (Open Table). Because I have a love/hate relationship with technology, I was immediately intimidated. But, I paid attention, I took notes , and I always took the time to practice with the system. My efforts to learn the system did not go unnoticed and I was asked to be the lead hostess during our soft opening. I noticed that this bothered some of the other hostesses that had more experience with this system than I did. But, the lead trainer told them that I was ready and I could handle it. From here, I continued to grow within the restaurant. I was given the most hours, with management leaning on me to make sure that the front of the house was organized and always ready to go. I grew from just one hostess out of ten to the lead hostess, from the lead trainer to the newly hired hostess team, and I was hand selected to help rewrite the guest services training manual. Within the two years I was at Ocean Prime, I was given three raises, making more money an hour than some of my counterparts with 9-5 jobs. Eventually, I outgrew this industry and found myself interested in the event planning industry.

I believe the reason I did so well at Ocean Prime was my ability to work with everyone on my team. I had no problem stepping up to the plate and completing any task that needed to get done for the betterment of our department and the restaurant as a whole. I would tackle problems on the fly and work to the best solution that would benefit the restaurant, the staff, and above all our guests. I built relationships with staff in other departments which helped all departments run smoothly. I utilized my interpersonal skills and was able to turn this job into a networking experience for myself and built relationships with many of our high profile regulars. I even secured a few job interviews from hostessing at Ocean Prime and people willing to vouch for me for a professional reference.

I have always been a social butterfly, and incorporating hostessing with my natural ability to be social has helped me develop a skill for networking. Anybody that knows me will tell you that I know everybody, my network is very extensive and it continues to grow on a regular basis. One skill set that many people lack is the ability to network and connect with others on a professional level. In today's society, it's not always about what you know, but more about who you know. I can name five different jobs that I have had over the years that I got offered because I or someone I knew had a connection with the company or the person hiring.

There are different types of leadership skills that would have to include tangible skills, and situational skills. Leading with both your words and your actions. Many people can talk a good game about what they bring to the table , and how they can help improve things. I like to be a woman of my word and when I agree to do something or make a commitment I back it up with my actions. Having great interpersonal skills and being able to connect with a variety of people is an important skill. When you get to college and the workplace you will be forced to work with different personalities. It is important you are able to work with easy going , difficult, and sometimes lazy people. If you lack the skill to work with different kinds of people than you are lacking in the leadership department and working with others or even leading others will be a challenge for you. And this could possibly hinder your growth as a leader. This skill has helped me learn how to work as a team, and deal with difficult situations in the workplace as well as in my personal life. I lead with a stern hand but an understanding/empathetic heart. I have led various teams and trained numerous individuals in my short time as a career professional. I have learned that when you show that you have passion for what you are doing and you care not only about yourself but others, it helps bring great results and gets everyone happy and excited to get the job done and work together doing so. Confidence is key. Being a leader requires confidence. You have to stand strong behind your purpose and lead confidently.

Always learning something new to enhance your skill set is important when you are evolving into a better leader. Currently, we are heavy into COVID-19 Quarantine, and during this time of isolation and social distancing, I have signed up for a few different online courses and webinars. Most of these courses are teaching me how to build my business and brand. I have learned more effective marketing skills, and I am teaching myself how to edit graphics and videos through various apps that big time companies use. The skills and knowledge I am learning right now will help me secure my dream job in the near future.

I have one rule that I live by when I am faced with a challenge or a life obstacle. I give myself a day to be upset and in my feelings about the situation. During this one day, I allow myself to feel all the feelings that this situation is making me feel. I cry, shout, feel pity all in this one day. After this day is over, I leave my feelings behind and work towards solutions to the problem.

For example, I had a temporary job as a special events coordinator at the Capitol Visitor Center (CVC). This job was the best job I have ever secured and a dream job to start with in the event/meeting planning world. I was making a salary and working at one of the most historic buildings in Washington, DC. Honestly speaking, the job was not easy, and at times, I struggled. Everything I did was not always up to par with my supervisor, and she called me out on it several times. Each time, I took her criticism and worked to improve. She did see improvements and applauded me for them. However, there were times when I would make small mistakes, and she could not stand it. When the time came for me to apply for the permanent position, I did so confidently. I went through the entire interview process confidently knowing I gave my all and tried my best during my nine months working there. On January 3, 2019, my supervisor called a meeting to discuss some new business. During this meeting, she informed me that I was not selected for the permanent position and that they hired two new people to join the event team at the CVC. When I first heard the news, I was so devastated, holding back tears while my supervisor was explaining. I had worked so hard to prove myself and secure this job and I still did not make the cut. Deep down, I knew that some of the decision was a personal one because I knew that my supervisor did not like me. I left the office that day and was so hurt. I went home and cried to my mom and grandma. Even though I was crying, I was already thinking of the next steps to finding a new job. The next day, I began reaching out to people in the event planning world letting them know I was looking for a new job. I updated my resume and began searching for jobs in Washington, DC , and New York City. This situation was not ideal but eventually, I found myself with a new job in New York City and made plans to relocate.

Working at the Capitol was an amazing job, and I just knew that I was automatically going to get the permanent position. I was too comfortable and assumed that I was going to be kept on board because of the time I had already put in. I was knocked down a few notches when I was told that I did not get the job and that my last day was in a month. From this experience, I learned that no situation is perfect. I also saw some faults in my performance, and I learned that when you think you are doing your best, always go 100 times harder.

Never be afraid to ask for help. You will never be ashamed for asking for assistance. In the fall of 2019, my current job at onPeak made some internal changes to the structure of our work teams. During this time, each office was strategically organized underneath the six directors across our three offices. During this time, I was overwhelmed with new accounts and more responsibilities. At one point, I found myself completely drowning at work on a daily basis. It got so bad that my director brought it up during one of our one-on-one meetings, and I completely broke down. It was then brought to my attention that I not once came to her and asked for help. My reasoning for not asking for help was because I felt like everyone on our team was busy and overwhelmed with their own accounts and that I would sound selfish for asking my team for help. I was then made aware that our offices were restructured in order for us to work more as a team than as individuals. Here, I learned the ultimate lesson of always ask for help even when you feel like others cannot help because you never know the solutions that may come. After that one-on-one meeting, I sat down and made a strategic plan to lighten my load at work and how the team could assist me with my accounts. My director was very impressed with my plan, and we made sure to begin executing it as soon as possible. She also reevaluated my current accounts and realized that I did have a lot on my plate at the moment. Asking for help essentially helped me grow into my position and get more organized at work.

No matter what you do in life you will always face challenges. And if you do not face these challenges head on you will not grow as a person. You do not grow in comfort, you grow when you are uncomfortable. But even in discomfort, you still press on. Remain resilient, and don't let life's challenges knock you down. In order to excel in life, you have to be ready for whatever life throws at you. Learning this has helped me to keep persevering in my entrepreneurial journey.

Never brag or boast about your accomplishments. You can be proud of your accomplishments, but remain humble and grounded in your accomplishments. As Kendrick Lamar says in his hit song, "Be Humble Sit Down !".

During my sophomore year in college I made a bold decision to move back home and transfer to a University closer to home. So after my Fall semester of my sophomore year I left Winston Salem State University and transferred to Howard University .Being a transfer student from one University to another can be a tricky situation. When you transfer, it is not guaranteed that all of your credits from your previous school will transfer. Some schools have different curriculum guidelines for transferring credits. Thankfully, I was able to transfer from Winston-Salem State University to Howard University and only lost four credits, equivalent to losing one class. Not only was I able to transfer and keep the majority of my class credits, but also, I was able to graduate on time with honors and no financial debt. So, I can truly say that graduating from undergrad was one of my proudest moments.

Currently, I am building social media, branding and networking consulting with my own program called Sydd in the City Consulting. I have been building my personal brand for over a year now, and I have grown a platform that has helped me build my new business. Through my platform, I have built a huge network of young professionals and ambitious entrepreneurs. I now have a total of five clients that I assist with creating social media content, managing their social media page, and enhancing their engagement on social media. This was not the original vision I had for Sydd in the City, but you never know what God has prepared for you along your pathway of life. So, I always try to remember that I do not have the final say so over my life and that God always knows what's best.

For as long as I could remember, I was always told that I was talkative. I would always hear from family, friends and teachers alike, "Sydney, you talk too much! You don't know how to shut up!". For a long time, I was put down for being a talkative person, and being called talkative was a negative thing about me that I really internalized. As I got older, I gained more and more confidence in myself and eventually learned to love everything about myself, including my talkativeness. I learned to take the negative connotation of being talkative and make it into a positive. I have so much experience talking my entire life that I am able to hold a conversation with any and everybody. I have used this skill and it has helped me network in different circles whether that is personal or professional. I believe this has, ultimately, led to my greatness. I used it when I was a hostess, I used it when I answered phones in the mayor's office, and I use it every day to help walk me through life.

Life can be challenging, but I take it one day at a time and I always try to stay positive through it all. I shine through my confidence and my go-getter attitude. There was no challenge that I ever turned away from. I always take things in stride and try my best to get the job done. Whenever I make a commitment, I follow it through and I always try my absolute best.

What makes me unique is my vivacious personality. My friends share the same love for me and that I am understanding of others and not judgmental. I am a 'tell it like it is' person, but I always tell it in the nicest way possible. My confidence is radiant, and I have the ability to uplift and encourage others by just being myself and leading with my actions. In short, I am a genuine person. I am far from perfect, but I take the lemons God presents me with, and I always find a way to make lemonade.

If there is any advice I can offer young ladies, it would be to be yourself at all times. Do not allow the criticism of your peers, friends, or even family to bring you down and to question who you are. The differences people will criticize you for are what makes you uniquely special. Always remember there is no other YOU in the world. Live in that truth and stand confident.

Anything you dream of you can accomplish. The skies are the limit, and you live in a time where your opportunities are limitless. Something I live by that I think has helped me in life is "The energy you put out in the world is the same energy you will receive back," meaning I always try to be positive no matter what. Everyone that I come in contact with I treat with the utmost respect, and I always give empathy and love. When you practice this, you will be blessed with positivity and love throughout your life. Lastly, love your fellow sister, and speak positively about your fellow female friends and family. For some reason, as young girls and women we have the natural tendency to judge each other and talk down about each other. We are stronger together than separate, so love your fellow sister and continue to uplift and support one another.

I am far from perfect but I make sure that every day I wake up I thank God for another day and I work to learn from the mistakes of the days past. I hope you were able to learn a little bit about remaining resilient and confident in your own natural abilities. Never give up on your dreams and if you have a goal work towards that goal every day until you can check it off your list.

I believe in you and I love you !

About Sydney N. Porter

Sydney Nicole Porter was born on March 29, 1994 in Silver Spring ,MD. Sydney grew up off Georgia Ave NW in Ward 4 of Washington, DC. Sydney began her collegiate career at Winston Salem State University but eventually she decided to move closer to home and transferred to Howard University, graduating Spring 2016.

At the beginning of 2019 Sydney decided to relocate from Washington, DC, and venture to the Big Apple. She moved to New York City in February 2019 and began working at onPeak, an event accommodations company. Sydney currently still works there, while pursuing her own businesses.

Outside of her regular job Sydney is the creator and founder of the social media platform Sydd in the City. Sydney originally created Sydd in the city as the name of her youtube channel to document her experiences moving and living in New York City. She never imagined that Sydd in the city would evolve into a platform that spotlights, promotes young professionals, and various businesses, brands, and services. Sydd in the city also offers event planning, branding, and social media management services.

Sydd in the city, She recently launched her online apparel line called Sydd's City closet which can be found on the Tee Spring website. Achieving multiple streams of income and becoming a self-employed entrepreneur is the ultimate goal and Sydney is actively striving to this **goal every day.**

You can connect with Sydney through social media:
Instagram:

Personal Instagram: @Sydd.intheCity Business

Instagram: @_CityConnections

Twitter: @Sydd_intheCity

Facebook: @SydPorter

LinkedIn: Sydney Porter

Alesha Wilson

"Greatness is a mindset. You must believe you are great." ~ Alesha Wilson

CHAPTER 5

YOUNG LADIES WHO L.E.A.D

IMPERFECT LEADER
By: Alesha Wilson

IMPERFECT LEADER

By: Alesha Wilson

I appreciate this opportunity to share some of my reflections and views on leadership. The goal of this chapter is to give a little insight into my journey, but most importantly to help you paint the picture to see the leader in you. Leadership is something I've never shied away from. As the youngest sibling of three and youngest grandchild of 12 I'm told I've always had that fire. I wasn't always as confident, but as I grew up I knew the best thing for me to do was to stand up for myself. I've always wanted to be that person that people would call on to do a task, ask for advice, or pretty much anything. I'm known as the *strong friend!*

There are many qualities of a leader and dependability was one of the first qualities embedded in my personality. Thanks Mom!! Other qualities I believe are important in a leader are strength, integrity, honesty, faith, courage, encouragement, and optimism. All of these qualities I'd say I strive to exhibit and continue to develop to be the best leader I'm destined to be. Take a moment to think about what qualities you exhibit. That leader is in you!

My earliest recollection of having a leadership title was in middle school as President of my church's Young People's Department and captain of the cheerleading squad. In high school, President of the Dance Troupe. In college, President of my school's dance company Mahogany, and after college, President of my church's Young Adult Missionary Society. These are all leadership roles, with associated titles. However, even when I'm not given a "title" I still strive to exhibit those leadership qualities in various groups, work spaces, and amongst friends and family. If you act with some of the leadership qualities listed above, you too are exhibiting leadership abilities, don't wait for someone to give you a title to believe and act on it. Be confident in your walk, talk, and actions and people will gravitate and follow your lead because they admire you.

Even though I've had a few leadership roles and titles, none of those make me perfect. Actually perfect has been quite the enemy. I used to rack my brain seeking perfection, it can be pretty stressful. Who likes stress? Not me! I've learned as a leader not to let perfect be the enemy of good. As a leader sometimes you feel pressure to get everything right, not make mistakes, have the answers to every question, and a solution to every problem. Throughout my journey I'm learning patience and to enjoy the process. We will never always be right and mistakes are meant to happen so that we can grow. Lessons can be tough to learn but I'm grateful for my transition and transformation. My advice, believe in yourself!

Learning and seeking knowledge has been one of the best parts of being a leader. I strive to learn as much as I can. Whether that be through continuing education, reading, research, talking to professionals, and even talking to those younger than me. I don't discriminate when it comes to learning because I believe if you're open and accepting, you can find lessons in pretty much anyone and anything.

There have been plenty of barriers and obstacles throughout my life. Some harder than others, some I felt I didn't deserve, but they've all helped me grow and I'm stronger because I fought through those times. When I have challenges, I sometimes keep it to myself because I don't want to be a burden to anyone else and I think I can handle it alone. You know that "*Superwoman mentality*"? I've learned through these times that it's ok to ask for help, that's why we were granted with friends, family, and even mental health professionals.

They exist to be there for us. It's ok not to have it all together, lean on your support system. Yes, even leaders need that extra push, you will not be alone in this journey.

As I'm writing this chapter for this wonderful book, I'm experiencing some very challenging times. Frankly everyone is, it's only the fourth month into 2020 and things have just been confusing, weird, and hard. I'm a firm believer in faith and the power of prayer. This time hurts, it's going to hurt for a while, but it will get better. Just keep fighting and we will see why! I believe *the why* is because God gives His toughest battles to His strongest Angels. Why me? Why you? It's not going to be easy, it hasn't been easy, but patience , time, and support will get us through. Find what keeps you motivated, protect your peace.

Now that I've poured my heart out, I get to tell you about some of my most cherished achievements. I am a proud product of Prince George's County Public Schools, maintaining honor roll status 1st - 12th grade. After I graduated from Bowie High School in Bowie Maryland, I decided to pack my bags and go to Florida A&M University (FAMU) in Tallahassee, Florida. To be honest FAMU wasn't my first or second choice for college. It was my big brother who convinced me to look into FAMU and my family took me on a tour to visit. We had a wonderful tour with Mr. Nance, the Admissions Officer, and the last stop before we departed was to "Ms. Olean's", a breakfast restaurant across from campus. We walked in, ordered our food, and the owner, Ms. Olean, looked at my mom and dad and told them "I'll take care of her". SOLD! That was the beginning to the greatest four years of my life. I enjoyed every bit of FAMU, the highest of seven hills!

My freshman year in college I joined a dance company, Mahogany, becoming President my sophomore year while I worked part-time as a Student Housing Leasing Specialist. With all my activities, I still managed to graduate Magna Cum Lade with a Bachelors in Business Administration. I wasn't exactly sure what I wanted to do after graduation, but I was always interested in entrepreneurship and business management. After graduation, I moved back home to Maryland where I knew I may be able to find a job. I later enrolled in an Event Management Certificate Program at George Washington University. I was interested in event planning but wasn't sure of the career field, so I decided to educate myself before pursuing. I learned a lot, met wonderful people, and was able to volunteer for many events for experience.

The last requirement for the Certification program was to plan an event from start to finish and submit a 60 page written portfolio. I decided to plan a prom dress giveaway for my community, similar to one that I'd participated in as a volunteer during my sophomore year in college in New York. This event, Once Upon a Gown, was an effort to provide students who may face financial challenges with free attire to go to their prom or special event. We collected a number of prom gowns, dresses, shoes, etc. and invited students from the Washington, DC, Maryland, and Virginia area to come get free attire. It was a great experience for students and I was able to write and submit a portfolio that satisfied graduation. Little did I know this one-time event I thought I was planning ended up being a bigger calling. From the success of the event I was encouraged to make it an annual event and expanded the collection to include tuxedos and suits.

After year two, I decided to start a nonprofit, The Right Fit, Inc. to offer our annual prom giveaway, Once Upon a Gown & The Suit Suite, for students and workforce attire distribution for career readiness. It's been a joy to serve over 300 students in the last three years and we continue to strive to help more because we believe that all students deserve the same opportunities no matter their circumstances. I've been granted the opportunity to speak on panels, TV and radio show interviews to share our story and have a positive impact on the community.

I'm currently in my last year of pursuing my Master's in Communication at Johns Hopkins University. It's been a challenging program while working full-time and running a nonprofit, but I know graduation is near and the reward is even greater. As I stated before, I yearn for knowledge and I wanted to learn more about the nonprofit sector to ensure I am most knowledgeable for the families I serve. Things change daily and knowing the best practices, tools, and resources to operate a nonprofit business is key to success. I'm learning that there's still and will always be more to learn. Don't stop learning!

There are a lot of people who believe in me and I'm so grateful for their encouragement and support. I've been granted a few awards: 2017 *It Takes a Village,* Awarded by G.I.R.L., Inc. ; 2018 *40 Under 40 Honoree,* Awarded by Prince George's Social Innovation Fund ; 2019 *Community Partnership for Programs and Services,* Awarded by Ivy Community Charities of Prince George's County ; 2019 *Community Champion,* Awarded by LAYC-Maryland Multicultural Youth Centers. Their recognition means the world and drives me to continue on this journey.

Greatness is a mindset. You must believe you are great. Once I believed in myself and built up the confidence to look myself in the mirror, smile, and say positively "I'm pretty great!" That's when it was defined. All the things I do, the awards I receive, the praise I'm rewarded – those are just an added bonus. The journey begins within. I stand up for what I believe in, work to be consistent in my behavior and build my legacy so that young ladies and men know how important it is to live to their fullest potential. I strive to be the one who people look up to, who people can depend on, who people respect, who people believe in, and who people will support. But I also realize I'm a work in progress, I'm not done yet, I have tough days, I need help, and that I'm growing exactly how God intended.

I could go on for pages with advice for anyone, no matter their age or gender. However when it comes to young ladies, know that you are a special human being, capable of literally whatever you put your mind to. You must work hard, because there will be challenges, there will be people who doubt you, there will be times when you feel defeated, but keep pushing. Write your story. You are the Author of your journey. Do it safely, protect yourself, stand up for who you are, what you believe in and just kill it! It will be hard, but the reward is even greater. You are stronger than you think, give yourself time and be patient with your brain and your soul. There's one of you and you are here to SHINE!

About Alesha Wilson

Alesha Wilson, an ambitious change-maker, founded a nonprofit, The Right Fit, Inc., in 2018. Its mission is to provide students who may be facing financial burdens with access to formal and business attire at no cost so they are encouraged to attend prom, special events, and are prepared for the workforce. The organization's belief is that no matter your circumstance each student should be granted those special experiences.

Alesha currently works as the Community Outreach Coordinator for Prince George's County Council Member Dannielle Glaros. This role allows her to actively pursue her passion for service and engagement in her community.

Alesha is currently pursuing a Masters in Communication & Nonprofit Management at Johns Hopkins University. She graduated *Magna Cum Laude*, from Florida A&M University in 2013, with a degree in Business Administration. Alesha is a leader with vision and drive committed to encouraging others to reach their highest purpose.

You may contact Alesha Wilson, President & CEO of The Right Fit, Inc. at 240-347-2467, info@therightfitinc.org, www.therightfitinc.org, Facebook & Instagram: @therightfitinc or Twitter: @therightfitinc

Tahjai Renee Ward

"Live with Purpose...Don't Quit...Keep Believing"... ~
Tahjai Renee Ward

CHAPTER 6

YOUNG LADIES WHO L.E.A.D

BUT GOD
By: Tahjai Renee Ward

BUT GOD

By Tahjai Renee Ward

Initially, when I first began, I did not know where to start or how to properly articulate how I am leading, excelling, achieving, or overall daring to be great.. This time gave me an opportunity to reflect on my life thus far. Also, to look at where I am at this moment. I dare to be great through this unseen burning fire that keeps pushing me to never stop and don't quit. Being great is my only option. I believe life is precious and God does everything intentionally. My life has become His and overall, I have become more aware and sensitive to Him. It is very important to look at something from the beginning to properly understand it now. Everything has a cause and effect.

Growing up I was raised by a single African-American woman. She did her absolute best in raising me. In a loving and God Fearing atmosphere. I attended Jericho City of Praise with the late Apostle Betty P. Peebles. I also attended Jericho Christian Academy until the 8th grade when I transitioned to Prince George's County Public Schools. It was a smooth transition for me because I had already received my foundation and tools so I knew it would be smooth sailing. I finished high school at Bowie High School and began my first year at Bennett College for Women in Greensboro, North Carolina. I was studying international business. I was just thinking about money and wanting to "do business". I did not have an actual reason or a plan, but God always has a plan. At Bennett I made some life-long friends who I consider as sisters now.

Fast forward to the summer of 2012. To be exact it was June 24, 2012, when God took over my life. He is the true author and finisher of our life stories. I missed church that day which is so unusual for me (I never miss church). My mother went without me. My cousin, who was at the house that day, stayed to look after me (praising God she did). I was complaining to my mother that morning about a bad headache. I was on my menstrual cycle and I felt extremely weak. This was not the first time I had felt like this. During my first year at Bennett, I experienced these severe pains, which I thought was normal. When my mom returned midday, the headache was still there. After praying and taking medication she finally said, "Ok, Tahjai, let's go to the doctors". So, we went to the doctors.

They initially said, "oh she is fine" and gave me more medicine. They recommended birth control to minimize the cramps". It was not until I was leaving, and was having uncontrollable urges to vomit did the doctor say, "oh this is not normal let's have her checked". After several tests including a MRI of my brain, they found I had a brain tumor located near my cerebellum and brainstem. It was the size of a golf ball and also, I had hydrocephalus (which is water on the brain). Unable to put an exact date on it, Dr. Timothy Burke explained it had grown with me from birth and this was uncommon. At the time I had just turned 19 years the previous month. Most of the time these diagnostics are more commonly seen in young babies and older adults. As a result, I had to endure more than ten hour surgery for the extraction of the tumor. There were several other surgeries that followed, praising God.

After three months in the hospital, I was transferred for in-patient therapy at the National Rehabilitation Hospital (NRH) in downtown Washington, D.C. I received treatment from occupational, physical, and speech therapists. During my time there at NRH and also at AAHS my grandmother rarely left my side. When she did, she had to go to look after my cousin who was in Indian Head, Md whose father was on tour serving in Afghanistan. Since I was not verbally communicating at the time, my family made sure I always had someone there who loved me. During my stay of over a month, I observed so much. Since I had just turned 19 years old, I was in the adult population of therapy. I felt so sorry for the individuals who had lost hope and were not actively participating in their therapy. I just was extremely eager to participate and do the necessary things that were required for me to get better. I had just started my life and this was not a part of my vision. As I was going through this time in the evenings my mother would spend the night. She would always feed my spirit with positive affirmations. Healing scriptures were constantly played on repeat. Of course, I found a church there at the rehabilitation hospital. My family and I would go every Sunday. After spending a month in the rehab learning how to walk, talk, eat, and do just about anything we take for granted, it was time to be released.

In celebration, my family and I went to The CheeseCake Factory (I love that place). This was a great moment that turned sour, on grandma's way home she was in an almost fatal accident where she had to get 12 T-bones and two rods placed in her back. The next day was my day to leave. However, I was feeling anxious and overwhelmed with the thought of something happening to my grandma. I was really not even aware of what had transpired. My mother received a phone call and asked the nurse to look in on me at this time. It had to have been after 11pm at this time. It was only by the grace of God that helped my mother manage and make it through an extremely difficult time in her life. Where both of the individuals she loved and who were the dearest to her was battling for their very own lives. My first day out, we went straight to the hospital. I could barely walk and stand up straight without holding on to something. I just had to see my grandma. I had received a wheelchair, but I think I only used it maybe two times. My mother drilled in me, "Tahjai never let anyone treat you like a cripple". That always stuck in my head. She reinforced that people will only treat you like you believe that you are. My hope came from my family and the love of God.

Through the process I understood that I was and still am chosen by God. He controls the winds in my sail. Where He will lead me, I will follow. When I was released from in-patient therapy I was transferred to outpatient therapy. I had to focus on speech, physical, and occupational therapy. All of my therapists were amazing. I appreciate each part they played in my recovery. Also, I guess I actually thought I would never dance again, but my mother reached out to Dr. Amanda F. Standard at Divine Dance Institute behind my back and expressed her concerns. I am glad she did because dancing gives me a chance to communicate and also was such a benefit to my therapy and overall recovery.

I believe I am leading, excelling, achieving, and overall daring to be great,by my choices to never give up and always being resilient against oppositions. During my process God gave me the idea of *Tahj Tees*. Which allows me to express my faith through apparel. My t-shirts have various uplifting sayings such as "Live with purpose," "don't quit", "keep believing, and "But God". I faced many intimidating and discouraging moments while I was trying to obtain my degree. However, I received my Bachelor of Science degree in child and adolescent study at Bowie State University. I currently would like to pursue more education in a graduate program possibly Entrepreneurship, Innovation and Leadership. My major during school changed to Child and Adolescent study. I realized that I wanted to help children by providing resources to families. I must continue to lead and dare to be great and continue to be a light in dark places.

My career goal is to become a child advocate. Being able to fight and speak up for individuals like young children is important to me. Young children are one of the most vulnerable in our population. Unfortunately, access to resources are not always available to these individuals, and I would like to provide awareness. Through all the things I have been through, I realize that God has a plan for my life and I want to help others realize that God has a plan for their lives too.

"But God"

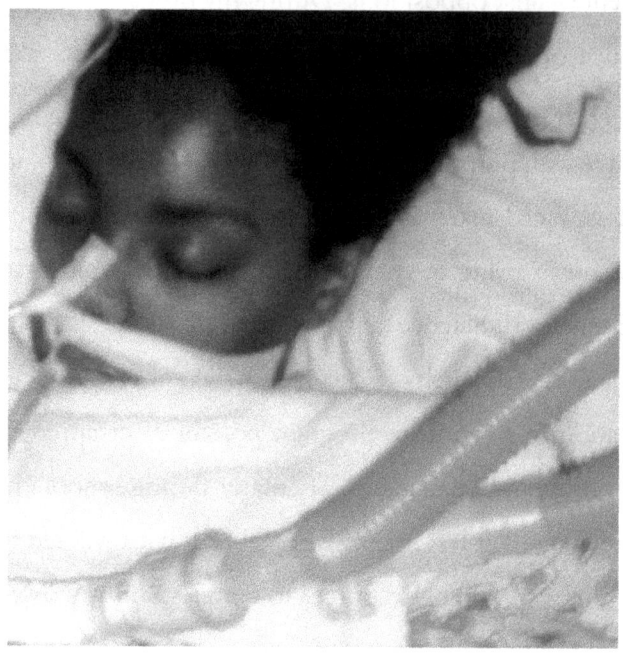

About Tahjai Renee Ward

Tahjai Renee Ward was born May 16, 1993, in Washington, DC to LaTasha R. Ward and Henry C. Frazier III. She was raised in Prince George's County, Maryland. At an early age of five, Tahjai loved to dance and joined the Jericho City of Praise dance ministry. Tahjai attended Jericho Christian Academy until the 7th grade. She entered Prince Geoge's County Public Schools (PGCPS) in the 8th grade and attended Benjamin Tasker Middle School. She graduated from Bowie High School in 2011 where she was a part of Future Business Leaders of America and the Student Government Association (SGA).

After graduating from Bowie, Tahjai went to Bennett Collegefor Women in Greensboro, North Carolina where her major was International Business. At Bennett, Tahjai was a part of the liturgical dance ministry. After completing her first year in college, Tahjai became extremely ill and had to undergo several surgical procedures to remove a tumor located in her brain. That area of the brain-controlled her swallowing, speech, balance, and coordination. Tahjai had to sit out several years for intense rehabilitation and therapy.

Tahjai relearned everything that most people would take for granted daily. Tahjai path changed with that life-changing experience Tahjai has completed and earned her Bachelor of

Science at Bowie State University with a major in Child and Adolescents Study.

ABOUT THE VISIONARY AUTHOR

Dr. Sharon H. Porter (Dr. Sharon) is an educator, best-selling author, publisher, and host. She is the Visionary Author and publisher of the Women Who Lead book series, the Next In Line to Lead book series, the Maryland World/ North Carolina Girl Book Series, the HBCU Experience Anthology book series, Class of 2017, What's Next, and Fifty & Fabulous.

Dr. Sharon is currently an elementary school principal in the

Washington, DC metropolitan area. She is the President of SHP Enterprise, the umbrella entity for Perfect Time SHP LLC, SHP Media and Broadcasting, Write the Book Now, and The G.R.I.N.D. Entrepreneur Network®. She is the Executive Director of The Next In Line to Lead Aspiring Principal Leadership Academy (APLA), and the Founder of the Young Ladies Who L.E.A.D. Mentoring Program.

Dr. Sharon is Co-Founder and Vice-President, Media & Communication of The What Now Movement, Co-Founder, Owner, and Editor-In-Chief of Vision & Purpose (V&P) LifeStyle Magazine, the Host of The I Am Dr. Sharon Show, and Co-Host of the V&P Inspiring Our Community Podcast.

She is a member of the American Business Women's Association (ABWA), International Women's Association (IWA), Professional Women of Winston-Salem (PWWS), Sisters 4 Sisters Network Inc, an official member of the Forbes Coaches Council, on the Board of Advisors for Envision, Lead, Grow (ELG), and a proud member of Delta Sigma Theta Sorority, Inc.

Dr. Sharon is a proud graduate of Howard University, Walden University, Johns Hopkins University, National Louis University, Winston-Salem State University, and a part of the 2019 Cohort of the Harvard School of Education Women In

Leadership.

It is Dr. Sharon's life's mission to equip and assist young ladies with the tools necessary to be successful in their endeavors.

You can find more information about Dr. Sharon at www.sharonhporter.com and can connect with her on social media @IamDrSharon on all social media platforms.

www.ingramcontent.com/pod-product-compliance
Lightning Source LLC
Chambersburg PA
CBHW070602170426
43201CB00012B/1907